More Dog Psalms

More Dog Psalms

PRAYERS MY DOGS HAVE TAUGHT ME

HERBERT BROKERING

Augsburg Books

MINNEAPOLIS

MORE DOG PSALMS
Prayers My Dogs Have Taught Me

Cover and book design: John Goodman and Michelle L. N. Cook
Cover and interior art: © Matthew L. Ambre/Artville

Library of Congress Cataloging-in-Publication Data
Brokering, Herbert F.
More dog psalms : prayers my dogs have taught me / Herbert Brokering.
   p. cm.
ISBN 978-0-8066-8042-2 (alk. paper)
1. Dog owners—Prayers and devotions. I. Title.
BV4596.A54B765 2008
242—dc22   2007036826

The paper used in this publication meets the minimum requirements of American National Standard for Information Sciences—Permanence of Paper for Printed Library Materials, ANSI Z329.48-1984.

Manufactured in the U.S.A.

Contents

Dedicated to all who believe God said:
"Let there be Dog."

Introduction

God said: "Let there be dog."

How pleased I am for the publisher to ask for *More Dog Psalms,* a sequel to *Dog Psalms.* God has planted many attributes into nature so it was easy to find more attributes in Dog that lead me to prayer and devotion. Therefore, this publication: *More Dog Psalms.*

These psalms are focused toward "peace making." The twenty-six devotions are prayers of peace. In this writing "dog" is guiding me to pray for kindness, reconciliation and the building of peace. If a 'lily of the field" can guide me to be less anxious then why not "dog" be an example for peace making.

Many dogs I have known help me feel and think toward peace: "If I have wounded you I will lick it and say I am sorry. I will sneak back to you, crawl back, come close, and touch you to make sure you know my heart. Say my name; do not be quiet when I repent. I know your reconciling voice. Touch me so I know we are making peace. Make me sure you will not permit a grudge to separate us. I am dog. We are face to face, heart to heart."

May these dog psalms show you more and more the many attributes of God embedded in creation. See in dog and tree and river and seed and wind and bird and sky the glory of God. May these psalms of the dog make you more and more a psalmist seeing all of life as language of God.

"I am dog. I forgive. A grudge will lead to isolation. Anger is my enemy; fear is a foe. I do not sleep well when we hurt. Forgiveness has the feel of stretching, a cool drink on a hot day, a warm blanket when chilled by rain, a safe pat after being chased by a predator." May *More Dog Psalms* help you see your dog in a new light.

Look again at your dog and pretend hearing: I am dog. I teach you the meaning of peace building.

"God, I know your word: Thou shalt not hold a grudge. Grudge is an enemy to peacemaking. Forgiveness is stronger than fear and anger and grudge and harm. Forgiveness breaks the strength of sin."

May many lines in these readings open up insights and peaceful vistas.

"I am dog. I am committed to you. I will keep my promise to you. I will do what we have agreed. If needed I will suffer for you, and be wounded in your stead. . . . There is a tie that binds us which cannot be broken."

I wish it were written somewhere in the book of Luke, "Consider the dog."

Herbert Brokering

Adore

I am dog. I adore. I look up with more than admiration. How often I have nothing to say. I stare for there is light around you. You are greater than I. I know this and I feel splendor. We each come from two worlds into this one another world. I am dog, made very good, but I am not the highest being. You are beyond me, whom I serve and obey. I need someone to whom I lift up my eyes. I dig a hole to sleep in; you build a house with stairs. I claim a corner under a porch; you give me a hand-sewn quilt on an oak floor. I lick an open wound to heal; you drive me to a dog doctor. I bark twice and jump in your lap; you hold me warm, close your eyes and pray. I beg against a screen cage in a dog pound; you carry me home in a basket and repeat my name. I am learning to adore. I am dog. I look up and you are more than friend. I am at peace.

God,

you made me to adore. I see beyond myself. I look in silence, admiring mountain majesty, springtime twigs and newborn fingerprints. My heart is dumbfounded by harvest time. I lift my eyes to hills with your children on all the earth who also live in awe. We all come with dim eyes; you heal our sight. You unveil and reveal as we stare side by side. You give rest and rain to just and unjust. You say who is perfect for you know our secret thoughts that we do not see in ourselves or in one another. You know what the old and infants do that makes for peace. You are a God of goodwill; we are created to adore, to look up and hear the song of peace and goodwill.

Test

I am dog. I test my limits. I know the ways of freedom are tender and true. I go to the end of my boundaries; I know the property line. I accept limitations I cannot cross. I do not climb trees. I know my limits and will test them. If I climb to the tip of the branches I fall. I will try once. I accept that I am dog and learn to live within my limits. I do not like living on a leash. There are true limits in my nature. I will find my limits and not be confined. I will not chase a lion but I will run. I will not swim the ocean but I will enjoy water. I will not be a kangaroo or zebra. I will not attack an alligator or race a gazelle. I am dog and will be glad to take a dog test. I will not study; I will pass the test for I am dog. Peace requires the truth.

God, *you set limits for seas and for rays of the sun. You have marked borders in your creation and lines we are not to cross. You put a tree in the garden to test our faithfulness to you and all boundaries for behavior. We are people warned and nations tested. You ask questions true and false, you set limits in laws of nature and rules for life with each other. When obeyed we have peace. Help us live without a leash. We are to live so all win and none lose, all pass and none fail, all hope and none fear. Take from us the fear of failing and fill us with the hope of peace. Take us to the very edge of creating and the making of goodwill.*

Respect

I am dog. I have rights; I require respect. I am dog. I am made to do what dog does. My history informs my spirit. Being dog is a long story. In me lives a deep wish. It is my duty to obey what I am born to be. I like being dog. I like my face, my tail, and the markings in my color, my hair. I like the way I walk, wag, wiggle, watch nature, romp, chase, am. I am dog and was born dog. I know the language of barking, the meaning of growling and howling. My story is a true story; my reasons are in me. I do as dog has done before me. People know me as dog, a living being. They look through chronicles to study me, respect me. I am dog, only dog, very dog. My nature is of old. There is none like me. I am what I am; I am dog. I cannot be otherwise.

God, *I am made in your image. You breathed into me breath and brought to life this person, this body, mind, and spirit. You marked me before my beginning with the traits of my ancestors. A genealogy is in me from those long before me. As recorded in scriptures I too am 'begat.' My spirit is of old and in my mother's womb you knew me. In me lives the miracle of being human. I have potential; I have limitations. I have no wings and I cannot breathe under water. I cannot fly with eagles or swim through deep oceans with whales. I do not bark; I cannot crow. I can reason, write, ask, ponder, calculate, meditate, moderate, will, create goodwill on earth. I know the language of being human. I know our long story. God, how you do give me honor. I know the spirit of respect. I am made a little lower than angels; so are we all.*

Reconcile

I am dog. I let go of my wrath. I do not nurture a grudge. I will wipe a slate clean. I do not plan warfare. See how close I stay by you. I expect you to not hold a fault against me. I am open to forgiveness. I look you in the eye and wag repentance. Stay with me eye to eye, heart-to-heart. Do not look away when I need to hear you voice. I nuzzle you and will not let the sun go down while anger is in me. If I have wounded you I will lick it  and say I am sorry. I will sneak back to you, crawl back, come close, and touch you to make sure you know my heart. See me return before it is too dark. Say my name; do not be quiet when I repent. I know your reconciling voice. Touch me so I know we are making peace. Make me sure you will not permit a grudge to separate us. I am dog. We are face-to-face, heart-to-heart.

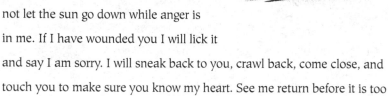

God, *I do not ponder or plan retaliation. Wrath and warfare is my enemy. I see you in the eyes of others so we are one family. From a distance I feel the voice and touch of another nation. The sun does not set on my anger; in the dark I seek to forgive and to bless so I have no enemy. I will not use the dark to harm those who call me their foe. I will try for a truce even before warfare begins. You have given us the gift of conversation, the spirit of reconciling and the miracle of peace. I believe in the power of peace that surpasses understanding. Wrath is the work of war. Reconciliation is the work of peace.*

Excel

I am dog. I can do more, still more and still more. I can excel. I am capable of finding land mines without being harmed. I am careful. My every step shows watchfulness, a special gift, and my excellence. I can capture drug dealers with my nose. I have a gift in me to do heroic rescues. I am dog. I can change the beat of your heart, lick to heal an open wound, warn you of a coming storm, and bring a child from a flaming room. I can excel in danger, in a beauty parade, on a high circus high wire, in a nursing home, on a lap. I am gifted. I can learn to win blue ribbons, be a best friend, and pose as hero before a camera. I can be the subject of a whole book, soften the spirit of a criminal, nurse a kitten, warm a climber on an ice ledge, run a sled race and win. I am dog; I can feel pride and with you win a gold medal. Excellence will make for peace.

God,

you have filled me with good things; you have made me gifted. Your own spirit is in me and I do in part what you do with power and glory. I can be to others what you are to me. Where there is danger I can save, where there is hunger I can feed, where there is a storm I can warn, where there is need I can be a hero. I have strength I have not tried and can teach what I have not yet learned. You have gifted me with passion I have not shown; filled me with music I have yet to sing and shown me excellence I have still to spend. God, there are land mines I have yet to hunt, races yet to win and wounds to lick. You created all things excellent and there was peace in the garden. Your peace is hid in all things.

Patient

I am dog. I will wait. There is a time to run and time to lie down; there is a time to bark and a time to be still. Time can go fast or slow. Time can stretch long and stand still. Time can hurry. I keep time; everything around me keeps time. I cannot hurry sunrise; I cannot hurry rain; I cannot stop rain. When the rain stops I will run. I will wait for you to come home from work. I learn to know the length of a ride, a morning, a mealtime. I know the difference between three hours and a weekend. I prepare for when you leave; I know by how you talk to me, how you look at me, how you shut the door, drive away. I go to my water dish; I know if you will be back soon or late. In this family everything has its time; I learn to keep my time. I am dog. Patience gives me peace. There are different kinds of time.

God, *sometimes I will not hurry. I will not run when I am already out of breath. I will not work when I am too exhausted. I will not lift what is too great a burden. I will go slowly. I will stop and rest. I may quit and surrender. I am not the timekeeper for all things, when to begin, when to finish. Peace requires patience. I am not in charge of time. There is a fullness of time I will learn to recognize the time we all keep. There is a right time for which I will wait. Patience will give me a new gait. Patience will help me see in all directions, feel feelings of others, know what to do next. Slow my feet and head and heart. Sometimes stop me to listen and look and hear what is right around me. Slow me down. Help me know what you have given that is in me. Walk me into peace.*

Decide

I am dog. I will choose to do. That is how it has always been; there is something I get to decide. When it comes to dog works I decide best. I am ready to be called into places where I can do the most good. Only I can hunt and rescue and dig and find with my ears and my good nose. This is how I am dog. I can quiet crying people, find the lost, guide the blind, save. Give me hard work to do and I will work. Send me into a disaster zone; I will decide where to run, when to sniff, where to stop, when to bark. There is work only dog does. I decide when the sun is high enough, when the day is dark enough. I tell you times of day, times of life. I decide when to run, when to hide, when to fight, when to growl, when to wean, when to romp, when to hunt, when to sleep. I decide from deep within where dog is dog. I watch the sun, the wind, the stars; I watch you. I will decide and you decide. I watch you watch me choose. There may be growling and then comes the peace. We choose together.

God, you have created me to choose. I can decide to do and not to do. I decide when to plant and when to reap, when to speak up and when to be still, when to shout and when to whisper, when to growl and when to sing. I know the disaster zones in the world, and will decide how I help and why I do not. I keep learning to say I will and I will not. There is a hurricane, I vote what to do. Death strikes, I vote; I experience sickness, divorce, loss, warfare, famine, flood and I decide; I vote. Miracles surround me, parables keep being told, and I decide if I will look to see them or listen to hear them. I vote. All those around me vote. I ask and see what they have voted, and the reason. May my growling prevent waging war. I will consider the meaning of all decisions for the sake of peace.

Honor

I am dog. I give honor.

I do not salute a flag. I salute you, your face, your voice, your presence, you. I will stand when you enter the room, greet you with dog protocol, and respect your every move. I will not act as though you are not present; I will give you worth for what you do that dog cannot do. You know a world I cannot feel and a world that is my mystery. You take me into your world as a best friend. I am dog; my world is a mystery. We see through the mystery and honor the maker of mystery. I honor you; you take me beyond yourself, beyond the mystery. I am dog; I bask in the mystery of being dog. You confound me with your being. I cannot salute you as you salute the flag. But I do respect, honor, and salute you for I am dog. I am loyal, respectful, graceful, tender, and great-hearted. I will rise when you enter the room, stay standing until you are seated. I will rise when you rise and face you. You are my flag.

God, *I have learned to salute, pay tribute, revere and give honor. I know the sacred feeling in me when I stand for elders and for people famed. The gift of honor binds us. I feel the feeling of peace when I pay tribute to someone who does not expect honor or even being noticed. The nod of the head to a stranger on main-street, a slight wave of the hand noticing a passerby feels like a salute. I notice them with more than a glance and I feel the beginning of bonding with them. It is hard to think of them as enemy; the motion of the hand and nod of head is a sign of honor, respect, and relationship. I stand before another until I feel the honor.*

Every salutation is a sign of peace.

Cheer

I am dog. I can be a cheerleader. If a howling breaks into the dark, I can keep it going. When it is too quiet I can start a solo in the dark. I can keep a Frisbee game running long after it's over. It is easy to turn a walk into a run, or a race. I can make you throw a stick once more when your arm is tired. I cheer you on with my heart and my tireless spirit.

Throw a ball into the water, I will bring it to you and not quit. You know I will keep the game going one more time, and then one more. I cheer the tired, the sad, the weak and lonely. One move, one lick, one nuzzle, one more look and you are cheered. I am dog; I cheer you on and you are satisfied with laughter. We are at peace; we both won. Now we are quiet together. Put your hand on my head and we will both grow peace.

God,

I did not know I could be a cheerleader, but I am. I am learning to cheer for peace. More and more I am out front, singing the songs, going through the motions, saying the right words over and over, shaping peace. People know that's what I do and who I am. Some are shouting louder and louder with me. Some sit silent. Some are on the other team with the other opinion. My cheers are no angry words. I do not embarrass the silent and offend the others. My cheers seek truth, understanding, compassion, prayer, reflection and petition. Peace does not come by anger and rebuke and harassing. Peace comes by uplifting the truth, the weak, the poor, and the tired. I will not quit what will end in love. I cheer with those who cheer me on. Peace is not grumpy. Keep us cheerful when we cheer.

Hope

I am dog. I hope. I hope for hours in silence, behind a shut door; on a doorstep I will wait, for you said you'd be back. I barked, begged; you promised. I can tell a promise that is being kept. My whole body feels when you are almost home, when you are almost awake, when we will soon take our walk. I am ready even before you say it is time. I bark when I hear the car in the driveway. I am in your way when you open the door. First you must notice me; then I will run ahead of you. If we will run or walk, I can tell. You do not ask me to follow twice; my hope prepares me to be alert, ready, half asleep, waiting, knowing for sure. You and I. You have kept your promise so I keep my hope. When you are ready, I am waiting at the door. I am dog. Hope is my bond. Your promise keeps hope from breaking. I am dog; I am ready to be with you. Who can ever separate us?

God, *my peace is rooted in hope. Peace is an old story. I wait for goodwill, seek it and expect it. Nothing will separate me from the hope for peace. Nothing in heaven or earth will destroy my hope and expectation. Hope is your work among us, a force at work to bring beauty and balance and life to creation. Hope is not wishful thinking. Hope is built on old truth, old history, and the old word: Behold, everything is very good. Hope does not allow for the work of destruction and warfare and hunger and separation. Hope sees the oneness in creation, peace in nature, the singleness of heart, the unity of spirit, the family of all people. Bind us together with hope; link us in ways so we talk together, eat together, walk together, dream together, work together, live together. When we lose our way to peace, bring us back together through the law of hope.*

Longing

I am dog. I long with all my heart. I do not make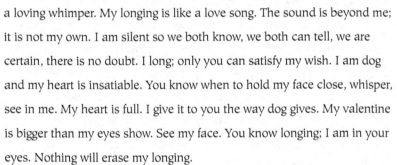
valentines or send roses or write love
letters. But you can see these in my
eyes, in my silence, in a bark whisper, a lick, a nuzzle,
a loving whimper. My longing is like a love song. The sound is beyond me;
it is not my own. I am silent so we both know, we both can tell, we are
certain, there is no doubt. I long; only you can satisfy my wish. I am dog
and my heart is insatiable. You know when to hold my face close, whisper,
see in me. My heart is full. I give it to you the way dog gives. My valentine
is bigger than my eyes show. See my face. You know longing; I am in your
eyes. Nothing will erase my longing.

God,

how my heart can long for peace. How my soul sometimes thirsts for a meadow with clear drinking water. There are in me songs of peace I have yet to sing. I know them by heart; I will sing them aloud. I will hear the hymns of peace around me and melodies beyond me. There are words and looks of peace near me on all sides. In the faces of needy and oppressed I see longing. I see the longing for rest, quiet, understanding, bread, good will, and peace. With psalmists and new singers I long; I want, and beg and wish. My heart is insatiable. Want has emptied me. Fill my longing heart with satisfaction. As you do this in me you do it to all your children. All want peace that comes when longing is stilled. We long; we wait and are fulfilled. We know the peaceful sound of your coming.

Marvel

I am dog. I marvel. I can be amazed, dumbfounded, and caught flat-footed. There are times I stand staring, eyes blinking, disbelieving, stunned, flabbergasted, and marveling. All you see is my silence; I am in a freeze like a mime. Still, like frozen. Slowly I move to show my hidden amazement and delight. I wag my tail, raise my ears, lift my head, and I touch you. One word can overwhelm me; I bark, once, barely. The marvel wakens in me: dancing, jumping, running in circles, frenzy. I marvel in silence; look, see the wonder in my eyes. I marvel in ecstasy. I like being overjoyed, amazed, and stunned to obedience. I am dog; there is much beyond me, outside me, within me that stirs marvel. I am not known to worship; not all is known of me. I am dog. I marvel and am fulfilled. My paw is touching you.

God, help us stand together on tiptoe and marvel. Help nations see dreams for each other. Show leaders the glory in other lands. Blink our eyes with what each other does and thinks and imagines. Turn our wonder and amazement into worship, so all hearts come together in a single will for grace and peace. Draw us to what is far beyond and is deep inside so we are overwhelmed. Help us move beyond our selves. Show us resources inside ordinary places, in the poor, the hurt, so we build each other up as sisters and brothers. These are more precious than fine jewels. Today I will reach out to touch someone in thought or word to show wonder and thanks.

We will be still that we may know you are one God and one peace.

Natural

I am dog. I am natural. I have not learned pretense. What you see is what you get. If I lick your face to wake you, that is how I am. I will scratch myself before dinner guests and wag against their feet while they sit in sofas. If they let me I will sit near them on a pillow as I do when I am alone. If the door bell rings I may bark in the middle of sacred story. They may think I am at fault; the doorbell made me do it. It is who I am. I have been known to jump against people with suits and silk dresses. It is my friendly way. They look down at me, smile, say my name; I jump. I am dog; it is my natural way. Guests are welcome to this house. If they come again they will know me. We will learn to know each other. I am dog. I

cannot do what they do. I am dog with all my heart. This is how I am made to be. I am created dog. Dog is my nature. I am here that we might have peace.

God, *your good news is my good news. Your gift of who I am is in me from the beginning. On every side are signs of who I am, who we are, who you are. I have memorized the story of who I am. I review the story of my nature. The garden of my beginning is a sacred place from my childhood. Often it was told to me. I see your peace in all that was to live around me. You made the garden and everything in it very good. The goodness and peace are hidden but not destroyed. Show me your peace in a wounded, warring world. Show our nations and neighbors how you have created us to befriend each other and all nature. Remove from me what distorts the goodness of others. Let not customs and perspectives of other people erase their worth and nearness to me. You know their hearts; you know them by name. You know who we are, how we are and why we are. Give us the peace that is shaped by our uniqueness, for we are many members and one body. Here I am Lord; you know me. It is so for us all.*

Remember

I am dog. I remember. I still feel how you saved me from the cold, how you fed me when hungry, touched me when I returned, held me after being lost. I remember and you will 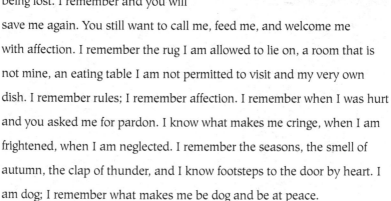 save me again. You still want to call me, feed me, and welcome me with affection. I remember the rug I am allowed to lie on, a room that is not mine, an eating table I am not permitted to visit and my very own dish. I remember rules; I remember affection. I remember when I was hurt and you asked me for pardon. I know what makes me cringe, when I am frightened, when I am neglected. I remember the seasons, the smell of autumn, the clap of thunder, and I know footsteps to the door by heart. I am dog; I remember what makes me be dog and be at peace.

God, you are a remembering God. You have built memory into creation. Seasons know when to come and go. Blossoms know when to bud and seed. You ask us to remember you and you will be there. This is how we stay near each other. In the clap of thunder, in the smell of springtime and a cry of a newborn we hear you at the door. In a sip of wine and breaking of a piece of bread we are at table with the universe and you are host. In a single thought loved ones in distant places, and gone ahead, are here. You have gifted us with the wonder of remembering. In the dark of night we remember in prayer those many who are foe and friend, those at war against our daughters and sons, and we remember them all in prayer. In remembering we find peace: the sick are near, we touch the weak, we forgive the enemy, and we dream with the old, we bless presidents and queens. God, we are your remembering children.

Prevail

I am dog. I prevail. I can hold out, out beg, out smart and out last. Surrender is not my strength. I prevail with my eyes, my bark, a whine, and presence. It will stay and not move until it is done. I will scratch a door to open until I have won, and I will pay the consequence. I will run until I am home. Though you tell me a hole is empty, I will dig until I am convinced with my own eyes and nose. If I am to follow a scent only you will stop me. I am insatiable. Deter me too soon and I will return tomorrow, to insist, persevere, remind you, persist. I am dog. I am made to seek, hunt, find and I hold my head high like a winner. So I see you at the close of good day: had a full day, feeling fine, got a lot done, good job, finished the work. I am dog; count on me to prevail.

God, I will not give up. You are a persistent God. Your mercy prevails, your love wins, and your patience holds out, your peace will come. Your spirit is in me; I too pursue peace. Peace is a power, a strength, a determined heart, a work. Peace is not neutral, peace is not surrender; peace persists, prevails, wins. I will follow the path of peacemaking, for it will take me through valleys and shadows and desolation and battlefields and hospitals and bombings and death. Peace prevails to the very end. Peace is the blessing that sanctifies life and the last breath. God, your peace is beyond understanding. Peace does not surrender or back off but enlists our minds and hearts to the end of time. Peace is the final word.

Peace has the final say for peace is love.

Forgive

I am dog. I forgive. A grudge will lead to isolation. Anger is my enemy; fear is a foe. I do not sleep well when we hurt. Forgiveness has the feel of stretching, a cool drink on a hot day, a warm blanket when chilled by rain, a safe pat after being chased by a predator. I cuddle without a word and come close with but a nod. Forgiveness gives me power, and I pass it around. My whole body shows forgiveness. It is no secret. Fear and anger hide; forgiveness is alive and is a force through my whole being. You will see me running with forgiveness from a distance. I have been waiting for the moment to bark and shake and paw when I am kindly. I know

what you say and do to forgive. In a single moment I know: a touch, a morsel, a kiss, a sound, a whistle. Forgiveness is the highest rule.

God,

I know your word: Thou shalt not hold a grudge. Grudge is an enemy to peacemaking. Forgiveness is stronger than fear and anger and grudge and harm. Forgiveness breaks the strength of sin, the chain of death and opens every kind of grave. Forgiveness finishes a war, makes foe a friend and saves life. God, your forgiveness relaxes, is restful, quiets panic and builds trust. My world needs your forgiveness, and for us to forgive one another and ourselves. O the power and the glory you have created in the act of forgiveness. Forgiveness drew the prodigal back home.

Forgiveness is your master key to peace on earth.

Commitment

I am dog. I am committed to you. I will keep my promise to you. I will do what we have agreed. If needed I will suffer for you, and be wounded in your stead. Do you know those many times when I would give you my life? If I hold back and do not guard you it is because the battle is too great for me. But in my heart I would defend you so that no harm overtakes you. My commitment is greater than my works. There is much I would do if I knew the way. I am dog and I commit the way dog commits. I keep my word; dog keeps a promise. Sometimes my great silence is my peace with you that is beyond my understanding. There is a tie that binds us which cannot be broken.

God, the cross is my sign of total commitment. There is a way that leads all the way. There is way for not backing off, not quitting in my heart. I will keep my promise as you have given yours to me. It is one promise and one commitment. I will do what we agree to do. If I am wounded in making peace I will go on. There is no battle too great for me. I will defend what is human and right and just with my whole heart. I do not yet know my limits; I do not know all there is to do. Tell me when I have finished. Show me some fruit of my works so I take heart and will not quit. If I am wounded make me well and send me on.

The way of peace is a hard road. I will be your disciple.

Obey

I am dog. I obey. Obedience is not a sign of weakness. I collaborate, cooperate. We agree with another. A joy builds in me when I obey. The obedience does not take advantage of me; it is a gift we have for each other. In a dog sled race, I obey. There are rules I have learned by which we win. I cannot win without you or you without me. Obedience is our yoke. To live in a kennel with others I will obey. I am dog. We eat from the same hand and are guided by the same yell. When learning to win a race I obey rules to qualify. I will hold the rules to the finishing line. To obey feels good and tastes good if it is a treat from your hand. Obedience knows a delight that is sweeter than candy.

God, teach me to obey. Kneel me at some rock and say in prayer "Your will be done." Give me a work in which I must obey to do the work well. Hold me close to you so our work can be done. Put me on my own while I am your apprentice. Jesus knew the steps of obedience. Teach your daughters and sons each step of the way, the craft of peacemaking, and the will to obey. Peace is not an easy work. Good will is crafted in all ways of life. We are in a race. We know the voice that cheers us along the run. Keep our eyes on the prize that is before us and is already in us.

Wander

I am dog. I wander. I go off on my own and gather burrs
in my fur. I do not notice soft mud rise above my feet; I only feel the cool
pond, moist bog, the pleasure I have now discovered. This is my time to
chase a butterfly and not be embarrassed that it escapes and laughs down
at me. Wandering is fun as I pounce on a frog that happens in my way.
This is not a hunt. I am dog meandering, on a stroll on a lazy summer day
or in a windy wintertime. I am dog-catching snowflakes that bathe my eyes
then disappear in the fall. I wander, noticing a family of birds and beasts
here before me. I wander; I sniff and know their names. I romp through
a maze of grouse and hare and mice and robins and
ducks who have wandered here before me. The
earth is a boundless garden of flowers and asphalt
and steel and woods where I meander freely, and
stray, and know my way home.

God,

I stray and I know my way home. I have peace and then forsake peace. Sometimes I wander through a maze and am lost; there are times the maze leads me to hidden meadows and nooks and niches that become vistas. Tiny places where I find the still voice of God. Thank you for the gift of wandering and straying and returning. You made me free to come and go, to flee and come home barefoot and without your ring. I inherit a new ring. There are far off places I know by heart because you have set my heart loose and kept me in voice distance. All the earth is a wandering people, pilgrims on foot finding the path to the one place where all can be at the table eating one food and drinking one cup and passing the kiss of peace.

Watch over

I am dog. I guard. I make safe. I will sleep with one eye to keep guard. I will hold my breath and count before deciding my attack. It is best not to engage in a battle I cannot win. I am dog and do not enjoy fleeing a foe in your presence. I too feel humiliation and do not like to be deceived. It is best to know one's own size and strength. Growling can be my best defense and ward off warfare. I have also found that wagging and the tail and a soft greeting can calm the air. The enemy may only be a curious bystander, or a friend you know whom I have forgotten. I am dog and I watch you to see if you need guarding. If not, I will stay sleeping or I will follow you with your friend. Let me know you are safe and I will stay asleep.

God, *you are with and in and among us. And you are over us. You are here and there and we know not quite where. Your rainbow is our constant sign of peace. All creatures, all creation, all people live under the one rainbow. You keep watch, you do not sleep, you protect. You are the one on high, the God on high over us. While you are in a manger of hay and a temple and two or three gathered, you are also over all. You are the blanket, the comforter, the cover in the cold, the dome of earth's cathedral and the seed before the oak. I too keep watch and shield and cover and protect and guard and keep. Night and day the world covers each other with intercession and kindness. Peace is a shield, a quilt, and the work of guardian angels. God, your own Holy Spirit is the great comforter from on high. Earth is filled with a spirit of peace.*

Lead

I am dog. I go ahead; I lead the way. I am often a forerunner; I plot, plan, and probe in my way. It is not a straight line for I know side roads and byways. I know the high road and the low road. I am dog and can run both roads at once. I know the slow ways that dawdle and we stand still. I know the fast slopes and fence lines and

we chase. I lead with all my senses; as birds migrate the sky I span the landscape. I will lead the blind so they see; I am a quiet guide who keeps you safe in a maze and you go as on your own. I am dog; I go ahead as a messenger, barking glad tidings that we are back home. They will know you are near for I have run to tell them.

God, *we all have forerunners, those who lead the way. There are the saints and martyrs who probed and loved and lived and died before us. They still lead us. They know a high road we have yet to travel. They rest in peace and their peace is still at work. We too lead. That same peace is our peace for there is one peace, your peace. We all run the race with a candle given us long ago, lighted at baptism. Make me a gentle guide who leads and does not chase, who goes ahead to show peace. I will skip while I run. God, I will lead from within, alongside as walking, ahead as a light upon the path, running as a herald. Peace is not just the end of the way; the journey is the peacemaking.*

Laugh

I am dog. I laugh. I can tell when something's a joke; I am dog; look close, I have a sense of humor. I like things that don't seem to fit. If you eat from my dish, see me notice. Curl up on my rug and I jump all around the room. Imitate my walk and I can go into ecstasy. Ride me on the handlebars of the bike and I hold my breath from laughter. I am dog. Pretend to bark and talk my language, and I tremble and wag with joy at your accent. You say one thing and I hear another; if you only knew what I am hearing you say. Our worlds overlap with the mystery of enjoyment. You go into detail with words and signs; I laugh. Your antics to me are full of oxymorons. You do not always know why or when I laugh. Listen, look and notice how much fun I think you are. You are my comedian in residence. My body is filled with joy.

God, *why am I so often laughing? Why do I have this sense of humor? What is your greatest joke? What is it that makes people smile the most? Is it the face of a camel or the feet of a kangaroo? Or is the joke your grace? Is love and grace and peace the big joke, the big surprise, the most joyful idea on earth? Your peace that passes all understanding makes the world smile and laugh and sing and praise. Peace is the great puzzle you have given your children. Peace is the riddle we are here to solve. God, you are theologian, gardener, judge, and singer. You are the comedian of the world. Sometimes we catch on, sometimes not, often later. Then we laugh. What does not fit becomes your rule. Sinners are saved; this calls for laughter. Grace is your great sense of humor.*

Peace is your big puzzle.

Heal

I am dog. I heal. I know when a wound needs a lick, when
a tear needs a snuggle, and when to come close to you. I know what is
too close and too soon. I am dog and will wait outside your door if you
are isolated. You know I am there. When you want good news I am your
good news. When you want thumbs up I look you in the face and declare
you well. I do not see you as sick; I see you as getting well. I bring a rag or
chewed bone to test your spirit. I am ready to play; you are not and I will
wait. I am dog and remind you of good times and how
we made it before. I cannot reach the medicine
shelf, but I bring you what the pharmacy cannot
bottle. I am dog, more than a prescription drug.
Medicare cannot afford me and I come free to
you. One whistle, one look and I am at your
side. Touch me, hold me and be well.

God, *I too make people well. I tend plants and feed birds. I visit sick, bring flowers you grow, tell them good news, and bring our one hope. We praise your doctors and thank your nurses. We learn the names of those who draw our blood and marvel how they read the meanings of signs inside us which eye cannot see. In surgery people from all lands in garments of blue and white surround us and serve to heal us. Though our lands are at war all healers together are your angels. There is no enemy in the room of healing. I am alone, a friend calls. I am depressed, someone comes to talk. I am sick; a prayer chain is at work. I believe, you make me well. God, the whole earth is of one mind; we all want to be well.*

Peace is also being well.

Judge

I am dog. I can judge. I can vote on how it is with you, your mood, and your spirit. Your tone of voice can slow me. I take one more look at how it is with you. I weigh. I am dog and I balance both ends. I see left and I look right and know the middle, the center. I am dog and you will not be confused or tricked. I can learn tricks but will not be tricked. You are innocent until guilty a few times. I can hold you on probation and make you accountable. Stay near me and grow honest. Walk with me and I will hear you; run with me and I will set you free. I am dog; I will be your advocate. Only ask. Peace requires a verdict.

God, *I vote. In my crib I voted. In my mother I did vote. I am made to keep going, to move on; there is a goal. I am on a journey and will not be tricked. I cannot travel this road without wisdom and judgment. Every turn and day I decide, vote, judge. I weigh which way to turn, which words to say, which cause to condemn, which work to support. I will make judgments with my spirit, with word and tone of my voice, with simple deeds. I will be held accountable; my heart will be a jury. I will listen, love, care, understand. You are my rock, my fortress, my Yes and Amen. I will be the same. You will give me words to speak. Run with me and I will hear you, walk with me and we will talk, stay with me and I will break your bread. When I vote, we vote. Peace demands judgment.*

Follow

I am dog. I can follow. I can tag along
and loiter while you will lead the way.
You can be in charge. I will dawdle,
linger, investigate, sniff my way,
zigzagging. I will hear you whistle,
calling me on, waiting, wishing me to
follow. You lead and I will follow. I am not afraid to
be far behind; you will not leave me. You know I will follow, eventually,
because when you are leading then I am not. I know the feeling of
following. The safe feeling of not knowing where I am going and you know.
You will not forsake me. I fall far behind; you call, I hear you but you do
not see me. I am not ready to hurry; you come back to find me, call me,
coax me, and lure me on. I follow the way I follow. On a leash I am close
behind you, at your side, or just ahead. On my own I follow, for you will
lead. When I do not know the way you know the way. I am dog. I follow for
I trust. We arrive together.

God, *I too tag along, sometimes dawdle, and linger but I will follow. You will not leave my sight. I will learn to follow on a way I do not yet know. There is a tomorrow I cannot see and a bend in the road I cannot know. The road may be severe. I will chart my journey; I will remember landmarks, mark milestones, record holy days. The way is well marked. Multitudes have traveled this road before me. Their footprints are fresh, benchmarks are set to song, old pilgrims keep stories alive, children still dance and shout hosanna. God, I will follow. I will stay close. My mind is a disciple's mind; I will keep my thoughts on you. You do not let me out of your sight. I do not know the way; you are the way. My feet are dressed in peace.*

Celebrate

I am dog. I celebrate.

I can move every part of my body at
once in a dance. I can make a little
go a long way. Give me a crumb or
a sip and I can make it a party. It will
look as though we have had a banquet together.
One pat and I will thank you forever. One word of kindness and
I will go an extra mile. A little is enough to keep me going. Throw a stick
and I will run in cold or heat and bring it to your feet. If I tire it is still party
time. I can go beyond my old limits if we are smiling. Laugh and I will do
an encore. Give me a treat and I will do two encores. Hug me and I will not
count the encores. I was born of a family tree that finds pleasure, and in a
family where we romped and tumbled the first day. We did not wait to be
invited to go to some playground. Our mother was our playground. I am
dog. Celebrating is an instinct. You are my peace candle.

God,

you created celebration. You began the work with a great light. We still light candles. We light them for birthday, birth, death, wedding, and the wake. Candlelight is the promise of your nearness and presence. Candlelight is the signal for a song and sacrament. One balloon and children begin the dance. We are marked to celebrate. Celebrating is a gift of the Spirit. All generations have sung their psalms and flown their homemade kites. Gloria in Excelsis is the song of children learning to read, of mothers musing, choirs rehearsing, lovers dreaming, babies nursing, angels singing, and people dying. God, in a piece of bread shared you have hidden glory, in a seed buried you have hidden a garden, in an acorn fallen you have hidden a forest; in Jesus you have hidden yourself. So be in me that I may be at peace in the world.